ROOTED
&
GROUNDED

ROOTED & GROUNDED

THE CHURCH AS ORGANISM AND INSTITUTION

ABRAHAM KUYPER

Translated and edited by
NELSON D. KLOOSTERMAN

Foreword and Introduction by
JOHN HALSEY WOOD JR.

Christian's LIBRARY PRESS

GRAND RAPIDS · MICHIGAN

Rooted & Grounded
Copyright © 2013 by Christian's Library Press

Originally presented by Abraham Kuyper as the Inaugural Sermon,
delivered at the Nieuwe Kerk in Amsterdam, August 10, 1870.
Amsterdam: H. de Hoogh & Co.

ISBN: 978-1-938948-53-4

Christian's Library Press
An imprint of the Acton Institute for the Study of Religion & Liberty
98 E. Fulton, Suite 101
Grand Rapids, Michigan 49503
www.clpress.com

Cover and interior design by Sharon VanLoozenoord
Editing by Chris Robertson, Timothy J. Beals, and Donna Huisjen

Printed in the United States of America

For Dr. Rimmer de Vries,

In recognition of your lifetime pursuits and enduring legacy as a cultural leader, economist, visionary, and faithful follower of Christ, who reflects well the Kuyperian vision of Christ's lordship over all spheres of society.

CONTENTS

TRANSLATOR'S PREFACE

Translating this inaugural sermon of Abraham Kuyper has been a most challenging exercise, largely because of its passion and eloquence. In this piece we hear Kuyper's heart speaking a language that some have described as baroque, language that suits both the occasion and his subject.

The arrangement of this piece into numbered segments is entirely our invention, as are all the notes.

The translated sermon you are about to enjoy owes its readability at many points to Dr. Harry Vandyke, who kindly reviewed the piece and suggested numerous essential improvements. Dr. John Halsey Wood Jr. also deserves our thanks for his thoughtful suggestions.

Nelson D. Kloosterman

FOREWORD

Although he is celebrated for his achievements in the academy and in politics, concern for the church permeated Abraham Kuyper's career and even preceded these other concerns. Kuyper's student days were marked by a master's thesis and a doctoral dissertation on the history and theology of the church. He then took several pastoral positions in the Netherlands Reformed Church, the broad national church of the Netherlands. Parallel to the founding of the Free University of Amsterdam and the Antirevolutionary political party was Kuyper's work as an instigator of a secession church out of the national church in 1886. He continued as an active teacher, preacher, and churchman in that church for the rest of his life. In fact, one of Kuyper's last writings was a series of articles on ecclesiology, which remained unfinished only because of his death.

This translation of Abraham Kuyper's *Rooted & Grounded* anticipates the publication of a larger collection of Kuyper's writings on the church soon to appear under the imprint of Christian's Library Press and by the generous support of Rimmer de Vries and the Acton Institute. The complete volume will include selections from Kuyper's doctoral dissertation on the theology of John Calvin and John a Lasco; various treatises and sermons, such as "Twofold Fatherland" and "Address on Missions"; and selections from larger works on the church, such as Kuyper's commentary on the Heidelberg Catechism, and his *Antirevolutionary Politics*. The centerpiece will be Kuyper's programmatic statement *Tract on the Reformation of the Churches*, which takes a unique approach to ecclesiology, particularly its development through the stages of church formation, deformation, and reformation. In addition, two interpretive essays will be included, one theological by Ad de Bruijne and one historical by John Halsey Wood. This larger collection by no means exhausts Kuyper's ecclesiological reflections, since they were so numerous, but it aims to provide readers of Abraham Kuyper and anyone generally concerned with theology in the nineteenth century and the modern period with a resource on one of the most contentious issues and one of the most dynamic figures of the era.

John Halsey Wood Jr.

INTRODUCTION

Abraham Kuyper and the Challenge of the Church

John Halsey Wood Jr.

Abraham Kuyper preached his sermon "Rooted and Grounded" at a time when the ground was shifting under the feet of the churches in the West. His sermon was, of course, not a comprehensive theological account, but he nonetheless provided in short compass an account of the church that answered the chief questions raised by modern society: What is the church? and What is its position in the emerging society?

Historiography of nineteenth-century theology, particularly Protestant theology, regularly treats the secularization of the mind, rationalism, as the primary theological challenge, especially when beginning with matters of Scripture and theological prolegomena.[1] Abraham Kuyper, however, perceived the main challenge facing Christianity differently. "[A] time like ours,"

---

1   For example, Claude Welch, *Protestant Thought in the Nineteenth Century, 1799-1870*, 2 vols., vol. 1 (New Haven: Yale U.P., 1972), 30-51; *Protestant Thought in the Nineteenth Century, 1870-1914*, 2 vols., vol. 2 (New Haven: Yale U.P., 1985), 213.

Kuyper said, was a time "when especially the church question dominates every other issue."[2] Elsewhere he said that the church problem was "none other than the problem of Christianity itself."[3] It should not surprise us, then, to find that Kuyper often thought in terms similar to Max Weber's and Ernst Troeltsch's "church" and "sect," since these contemporaries were likewise concerned with the church question.[4]

Social changes, as much or more than intellectual ones, caused trouble for the church. Mass, democratic culture, the separation of church and state, and religious pluralism were particularly difficult to deal with. The "church question" arose amid the transition in Western society that Charles Taylor calls the transition from the "ancien régime" to the "Age of Mobilization," that is, from an organically and hierarchically connected society to a fragmented society based on mass participation, charismatic leaders, and organizational tactics.[5] Abraham Kuyper was a key instigator in this cultural transformation as the populist organizer of the Netherlands' first modern political party (and eventually Prime Minister), as a newspaper editor who used modern media to educate and mobilize his popular base, as one who broadened enfranchisement in church and political society, and as the founder of the Free University of

---

2   *"Rooted & Grounded,"* 22.

3   Abraham Kuyper, "Conservatism and Orthodoxy: False and True Preservation (1870)," in *Abraham Kuyper: A Centennial Reader*, ed. James D. Bratt (Grand Rapids: Eerdmans, 1998), 69. See also, "De Sleutelen," in *Uit Het Woord. Stichtelijke Bijbelstudiën* (Amsterdam: J. A. Wormser, n.d.), 41-42.

4   See the discussion of church and culture in "Common Grace (1902-4)," in *Abraham Kuyper: A Centennial Reader*, 187-97.

5   Charles Taylor, *A Secular Age* (Cambridge, Mass.: Harvard U.P., 2007), 423-72. See also Joris van Eijnatten and Fred van Lieburg, *Nederlandse Religiegeschiedenis* (Hilversum: Verloren, 2005); Hugh McLeod, *Religion and the People of Western Europe, 1789-1970* (Oxford: Oxford U.P., 1981), 17-18; Peter van Rooden, "Long-Term Religious Developments in the Netherlands, c. 1750-2000," in *The Decline of Christendom in Western Europe, 1750-2000*, ed. Hugh McLeod and Werner Ustorf (Cambridge: Cambridge U.P., 2003), 121-22.

Amsterdam, the Netherlands' first private university.[6] Before any of these things, however, Kuyper was a pastor in the Dutch Reformed Church, and in the transition to the Age of Mobilization, the Dutch Reformed Church (*Nederlandse Hervormde Kerk* or *NHK*, also referred to as the national church or *volkskerk*) faced an unprecedented problem, as historians Fred van Lieburg and Joris van Eijnatten explain: "orphaned by the withdrawing of the state and no longer obvious symbol of the existing order, the church needed a new legitimation."[7] The church would have to "go Dutch," so to speak. It would have to pay its own way, metaphorically and in some respects literally.[8]

Abraham Kuyper's sermon "Rooted and Grounded" dealt with this new situation that had emerged over the course of the nineteenth century. The Dutch Reformed Church never enjoyed the numerical dominance that the national churches of Scandinavia did, for example; nonetheless it was a privileged and a public church in Dutch society, a status that many were loath to give

---

6 Various studies have dealt with Kuyper and themes of the mobilization of Dutch society: David Bos, *Servants of the Kingdom: Professionalization among Ministers in the Nineteenth-Century Netherlands Reformed Church* (Leiden: Brill, 2010); James Bratt, "Abraham Kuyper's Public Career," *Reformed Journal* 37 (1987): 9-12; "Kuyper and Dutch Theological Education," in *Theological Education in the Evangelical Tradition*, ed. R. Albert Mohler and D. G. Hart (Grand Rapids: Baker, 1996); George Harinck and Lodewijk Winkeler, "De Negentiende Eeuw," in *Handboek Nederlandse Kerkgeschiedenis*, ed. Herman J. Selderhuis (Kampen: Kok, 2006); Jeroen Koch, "Abraham Kuyper Tussen Gereformeerde Natie en Gereformeerde Zuil," *Tijdschrift voor Geschiedenis* 120 (2007); G. J. Schutte, "Abraham Kuyper: Vormer van een Volksdeel," in *Het Calvinistisch Nederland: Mythe en Werkelijkheid* (Hilversum: Verloren, 2000); van Eijnatten and van Lieburg, *Nederlandse Religiegeschiedenis*; Michael Wintle, "Protestant Dominance and Confessional Politics: Switzerland and the Netherlands," in *The Cambridge History of Christianity: World Christianities, c. 1815-1914*, ed. Sheridan Gilley and Brian Stanley (Cambridge: Cambridge U.P., 2006); *An Economic and Social History of the Netherlands, 1800-1920: Demographic, Economic, and Social Transition* (Cambridge: Cambridge U.P., 2000); James C. Kennedy, *Stad op een Berg: De Publieke Rol van Protestantse Kerken* (Zoetermeer: Boekencentrum, 2009).

7 van Eijnatten and van Lieburg, *Nederlandse Religiegeschiedenis*, 274.

8 See John Halsey Wood Jr., *Going Dutch in the Modern Age: Abraham Kuyper's Struggle for a Free Church in the Netherlands*, ed. David Steinmetz, Oxford Studies in Historical Theology (New York: Oxford U.P., *forthcoming*).

up.[9] In 1816, King William I had taken the loose confederation of Dutch Reformed churches and combined them into a single administrative unit under the national synod, reflecting the centralizing tendencies of the post-Napoleonic era. A governmental department of public worship oversaw church life in the Netherlands. Pastors, including Abraham Kuyper, were often paid by the government. The state universities housed the departments of theology, and they were the only permissible educational institutions for prospective ministers in the national church. Besides the Dutch Reformed Church, the Roman Catholic Church and several smaller communions, such as the Lutheran and Remonstrant churches, were tolerated and even received some support from the state, but they did not enjoy the public prestige of the *NHK*. The *NHK* was, therefore, an established church, but not a state church insofar as it was not the sole church sanctioned by the state. Nonetheless, the Dutch Reformed Church was so closely tied to national life that when a small group of dissenters broke away from the church in 1834, soldiers were quartered in dissidents' houses, and minister Hendrik de Cock was imprisoned.[10] A break with the national church was a matter of national security, especially after the separation of Belgium, with its Roman Catholic majority, from the Dutch federation.

Constitutional disestablishment and religious freedom were important turning points in the transition from the ancien régime. In 1848, the Netherlands definitively achieved disestablishment, earlier than many of its neighbors. Correlatively, whereas most European theologians still believed in the unity of church and state at the end of the nineteenth century,[11] Kuyper

---

9 See van Rooden, "Long-Term Religious Developments," 113-29; Harinck and Winkeler, "De Negentiende Eeuw," 597-721.

10 A. J. Rasker, *De Nederlandse Hervormde Kerk Vanaf 1795* (Kampen: Kok, 1974), 64-66; Karel Blei, *The Netherlands Reformed Church, 1571-2005*, trans. Allan J. Janssen, The Historical Series of the Reformed Church in America (Grand Rapids: Eerdmans, 2006), 55-70.

11 Welch, *Protestant Thought*, vol. 2, 213.

did not, but that meant there was little theological precedent to go on. Granting the separation of church and state, many in the *NHK* still aspired to be a national church. While not a state sponsored church, a national church would nonetheless be a church uniquely responsible for the whole of the Dutch people. Many continued to champion the *volkskerk* (i.e., national church) ideal in the late nineteenth century,[12] but disestablishment and a growing consciousness of the religious pluralism of the Dutch people made that ideal ever more difficult to imagine.

Commenting on Taylor's account of the Age of Mobilization, Clark Gilpin says that the problem was "how would persons experience transcendence when the most immediate experience of religious participation arose from personal choice or agency?"[13] The church problem was, in fact, not a single problem but a set of interrelated problems brought on by the new era. First, as Gilpin suggests, there was the problem of the human and the divine. Disestablishment and democratizing trends, which Kuyper championed, remade the churches into voluntary institutions. That called into question the heretofore assumed givenness of the church and raised the question of whether and how the church could be simultaneously a divine and a human institution. Related to this was the question of belonging versus belief. If one did not simply belong to the church by virtue of Dutch national or ethnic heritage, then might not one freely choose the church that best satisfied one's own convictions, or perhaps opt out altogether? Finally, modern society questioned Christianity's, and especially the church's, public role. If the church was no longer sponsored by public institutions like the state but grounded in subjective choices, did it have any remaining public

---

12 Annemarie Houkes, *Christelijkevaderlanders:Godsdienst,Burgerschap,en De Nederlandse Natie (1850-1900)* (Amsterdam: Wereldbibliotheek, 2009), passim.

13 William Schweiker, W. Clark Gilpin, and Willimein Otten, "Grappling with Charles Taylor's *A Secular Age*," *Journal of Religion* 90 (2010): 387.

significance at all? These questions formed the social and theological milieu addressed in "Rooted and Grounded."

In this address, Kuyper offered an ecclesiological paradigm to meet the exigencies of modern society. The church, he said, was at once an organism and an institution. As rooted, the church had an inner organic life that flows directly from the Spirit of God. The way to understand this aspect of the church was the various biological metaphors used in Scripture, especially the church as a body. This would also explain the familial character of the church. Whatever disestablishment may signify, the church is not a mere club but makes claims even upon those born to its bosom apart from any deliberate choice. Nevertheless, the life of the church was not to be taken for granted, as perhaps a national church was prone to do. It must be deliberately built. The church was not only a body but also a house, and as such it was founded and built by human hands. This building had a solid outward form that shaped and protected the inner organism. "The church is called a multitude of priests, legitimated through birth but consecrated only through anointing," he said.[14]

Moreover, these two, the hidden mystical life and the outward form, were not to be separated but existed in a reciprocal dependence. In another metaphor, Kuyper likened the church to the spontaneous force of a river that would nonetheless dissipate were it not for the banks that held it. This was a sacramental vision of the church. What Avery Dulles said about sacramental ecclesiology in the twentieth century—"The corporal expression gives the spiritual act the material support it needs in order to achieve itself; and the spiritual act gives shape and meaning

---

14 *"Rooted & Grounded,"* 5.

to the corporal expression"—neatly fits the way Kuyper had described the church a century before.[15]

The religious pluralism of the day was nowhere more apparent than in the Dutch Reformed Church itself: Kuyper, with his sacramental ecclesiology, over against several other alternatives struggling for dominance in that church. The Hegelian option championed by modernist Protestants held that the institutional church's days were coming to an end. Henceforth the state, not the church, would be the chief ethical institution of humanity and the spiritual life of humanity would dissipate into society at large. At the other end of the spectrum, revivalists, for all their spiritual vigor, championed a similarly mystical spirituality that demolished institutional religion. Then there were those who maintained the historic institution but with too little regard for the church's spiritual vitality, like the conservatives who were satisfied with the status quo and unwilling to make an indecorous scene at a proper ecclesiastical table.

Kuyper's sacramental ecclesiology also included a social ethic. The basis for this ethic was the same as for Augustine's two cities: the distinction between God and humanity. Like Augustine, Kuyper called for a separation of the societies determined by these two principles. "'Consecrated and unconsecrated' or 'everything alike,' that is the question that either inflames our love for the church or cools it, and that must determine her right of existence." Between these two ethics, Kuyper decidedly chose the first. As a result, Kuyper's "free church" would be one that was free from the attachment to money (and presumably, from the spiritual lethargy that economic stability induces); free from an ecclesiastical hierarchy; and most importantly, free from the state. This created a certain paradox in the church's social ethic. As a divine institution, the church was not a mere club, and yet the state would live by the fiction that it was. Troeltsch captured this paradox of the free church: "at least outwardly, the

---

15 Avery Dulles, *Models of the Church* (New York: Doubleday, 1987), 58.

form of Church-order becomes that of a voluntary association, even though theologically the community which thus comes into being may still continue to be considered as an objective, ecclesiastical institution."[16] The effects for Kuyper were a more distanced relationship between the church and other public entities like nation and state, and greater suspicion towards the encroaching secular society.

Although Abraham Kuyper's organism—institution ecclesiology—bears the marks of its day, it remains remarkably timely. From every church nave, there is the call today to be "spiritual but not religious." Some like Harvey Cox (liberal Protestant) and Diana Butler Bass (evangelical Protestant) are positively exultant about that.[17] Both predict the supplanting of the church by a more individualistic and free-forming Jesus-religion. They hope for a recovery of the "lost Christianities" of the second-century Gnostics. Others, like Ross Douthat (Roman Catholic), subtitle their books with phrases like "how we became a nation of heretics," and using much the same empirical data as their antagonists, they lament the loss of an identifiable center for Christianity.[18] Whatever their differences, both groups agree that some form of Jesus-mysticism is ascendant in the modern West. This is not completely surprising, since other institutions, particularly the omni-competent state and the amorphous market, have taken over the role as the prime meaning-making institutions in society, leaving the churches lying somewhat confused on the therapist's couch.

As one who had multiple conversion experiences, Abraham Kuyper knew firsthand the mystical side of Christianity. The

---

16 Ernst Troeltsch, *The Social Teaching of the Christian Churches*, trans. Olive Wyon, 2 vols., vol. 2, Library of Theological Ethics (Louisville: Westminster/John Knox, 1960), 656.

17 Diana Butler Bass, *Christianity after Religion: The End of the Church and the Birth of a New Spiritual Awakening* (New York: HarperOne, 2012); Harvey Cox, *The Future of Faith* (New York: HarperOne, 2009).

18 Ross Douthat, *Bad Religion: How We Became a Nation of Heretics* (New York: Free Press, 2012).

organic, or "rooted" side accounted for the unaccountable work of the Spirit, but Kuyper also saw the excesses to which unrestrained mysticism could lead—"the draining away of our lifeblood as a result of spiritualism." In Paul's account in Ephesians, Kuyper found biblical warrant for both the mystical and the institutional, external, public nature of the Christian church. If Cox, Bass, and Douthat are to be believed, it is the "grounded" nature of the church that needs shoring up. Institutional forms like creeds, which provide Christians with the common reference point necessary for life together and by which they can make a shared witness to the world, are the most threatened by the emerging religious culture.

"Rooted and Grounded"
(Ephesians 3:17c)

AUTHOR'S PREFACE

The subjects I spoke about to the church on the occasion of my departing from Utrecht and coming to Amsterdam are dominating the ecclesiastical situation.

Orthodoxy is defending itself, laying its hand on a good that the spirit of the age wants to destroy. This makes orthodoxy conservative. But this is the question: Is orthodoxy fighting for a life principle, or merely for a few incidental consequences deduced from this principle?

If the former, then orthodoxy will live. If the latter, it will die.

There are only two principles that carry within themselves a characteristic world, an entirely distinctive world: eternal election and humanism. As long as orthodoxy does not choose between them with self-conscious decisiveness, through its own fault it is leaving David's sling lying unused, the very weapon it possesses with that tremendous principle of "election," according to Scripture and Augustine and Calvin.

Against such conservatism that preserves only the incidental consequences while surrendering the principle, I have given warning in my farewell address.[1]

In this my inaugural address, I sought to arouse my listeners to return to the church's distinctive principle.

If the church has a characteristic life principle, then—but only then—that life must manifest its independence in terms of essence and form.

Both the denial of the church's characteristic organism and the failure to maintain the church's characteristic institution[2] betray a vacillation in the choice placed before every heart, the choice that at its deepest point exists between "election" and "humanism."

At the close of the 42nd chapter of his oracles, Ezekiel describes the wall that had been erected "to make a separation between the sanctuary and the profane place" [Ezek. 42:20; KJV].

That wall does not merely consist in the acknowledgment of "sin," not merely in the acceptance of "miracles," but first of all includes "election."

---

1 (Original note: Although the publisher preferred to issue this as a separate publication, I nonetheless wish that the mutual connection between these two addresses might not be overlooked. The farewell sermon [given in Utrecht, 31 July 1870, entitled *Conservatisme en Orthodoxie*] has appeared simultaneously, also published by Messrs. H. de Hoogh & Co.) See the English translation of this sermon: "Conservatism and Orthodoxy: False and True Preservation (1870)," in *Abraham Kuyper: A Centennial Reader*, edited by James D. Bratt (Grand Rapids, Michigan: Wm. B. Eerdmans, 1998), 65-85.

2 The key Dutch word *instituut* can mean *institution, institute, agency, department*, or *office*, depending on its context (cf. *Van Dale Groot woordenboek Nederlands-Engels*, fourth edition [Utrecht, 2008], s.v. "instituut"). Despite the somewhat common usage of the phrase "the church as *institute*," in the interests of uniformity with other contemporary English translations of Dutch theological works, we will use the term *institution* in agreement with the prevalent rendering employed in Herman Bavinck's *Reformed Dogmatics*, volume 4: *Holy Spirit, Church, and New Creation* (Grand Rapids: Baker Academic, 2008), chapter 6, "The Church's Spiritual Government" (326-388, esp. §497, 329-332).

The church must live from the confession of these facts; her form must be the expression of those facts.

All issues relating to the church question must be decided by the acceptance or rejection of these principles. Therefore I thought that I ought intentionally to examine the effort of so many in our time who seek to escape the difficulty of the situation, either by denying the principle of the church's characteristic life or by destroying the necessary connection between organism and institution.

Everything depends here on making the proper distinction: the only true principle lies in *orthodoxy*, but the conservatives in this country are impotent to the extent that they are not living from this principle; whereas through the activities of their lives the *non-conservatives* are exercising an unmistakable influence, but one that ultimately dissipates because they are not consolidating the roots of that life in the true principle.

It is the nature of the case that the limited space of an ecclesiastical address excludes any attempt at completeness.

For that reason I nevertheless thought that what was spoken should not be kept private.

Only by publishing these addresses will those whom I oppose have a chance to critique me.

Kuyper

Amsterdam
10 August 1870

1

The Need of the Hour: A Church That Is Both Organism and Institution

L ET MY BEGINNING among you, Gentlemen, be "in the name of the Father and the Son and the Holy Spirit," and as is fitting with such a glorious confession, I do so with quiet apprehension and yet with unshakable confidence. Accept then my testimony that I come to you with my whole heart, even as I have already bound myself to you in this very house of prayer with the sobriety of uprightness. I ask only this: Do not require that already now I celebrate in a happy mood that bond with your congregation. At the moment such happiness is impossible for me, since the farewell to so many long-time friends has only just faded from my lips. Were I able to rejoice already now, either my testimony of pain to them or my display of joy to you would have to be mere pretense, betraying a shallow heart in which pain and joy could displace each other so quickly. For that reason, no matter how warmly I thank you for the love with which you have already greeted me, no matter how much within your congregation appeals to me, let the requirement of the heart, I pray of you, run its course for the present, and bear with me as I accept my ministry in your midst with sedate sobriety and quiet gravity.

With respect to only one thing I will not suppress my joy even now, namely, that having arrived in your midst, I may come after being called by you. It is good for me that the free choice of the congregation itself commissioned me with this ministry, so that the foundation of my endeavor rests not in any outside body, but in you yourselves. I know very well that with such a choice not everybody had desired my perspective, and even if united in perspective, not everybody took delight in my person; but I also know that this has repeatedly been the case with every choice made by free people. In this regard the significance of that free vote is not at all being minimized in my estimation. Even in this way the election of the congregation is the license from which I derive the right to labor among you. Through it I am standing on firm ground and the way to trust has been paved. Precisely through that choice I enjoy an uncoerced relationship to the congregation, and because I have never made a secret of my ideas, I know through that election what the congregation expects from me.

Do not think, however, that I am therefore glossing over the risk that lies embedded in this new legal situation [rechttoestand]. I sense deeply that this new method of election bears within its bosom a new church, and here too the birth pangs are not coming without pain and danger. Every transition is already stressful, so why not also a turn of events such as the one we have witnessed so suddenly, so completely, in our denomination? We have left the ancient paths, but everyone is asking: Where are we headed? This explains the linguistic confusion that is so disastrous, a befuddlement so regrettable, an error so dangerous, all of which are currently disturbing us in every controversy in our ecclesiastical life. We know that from which we have partially escaped and will one day entirely escape, but who will focus our eyes on a firm, unshakeable goal, and who will pioneer the way leading us with certainty through this morass of confusion to that goal? Moreover, in those surging billows of our ecclesiastical life, where does the fixed position lie from which moral power can be exercised without an arrogance that excludes compassion, without a passion that makes one unfair, even more, without that reckless rashness that corrupts everything, because it will drive us past our goal?

This is what people are asking, and the cacophony of voices that arises when the question is asked is confusing. But still, if we listen carefully, then three distinct voices can be heard above the others in that swirl of sounds. *Over here* people want the church to flow out into society, while *over there* they want the church revamped in line with Rome, and *over yonder* they want to make the church expand into the free church of our time.

The one cries out: Away with the church, as institution or organization! Christian living must continue only as an organism. "You must increase, I must decrease," is the humble testimony thought fitting for the church to bring to society. Flowing out into the state must be the goal of Christianity, and therefore if one day the state takes to its own bosom what initially the church alone provided, that church will inevitably cease.

But no, we want nothing of that super-spirituality that dissipates everything!, cries another voice. Jesus' church must become for us not an organism, but preeminently an organization, above all an institution. Therefore Rome's model is being investigated once again, to revive not Rome's abuses but Rome's church. For one of two things must be true: either let it become once again a church that does not rest in the human race but is laid firmly and immovably upon the human race, or what you wanted to stamp with the name of church is unworthy of that sacred name.

A third group, finally, just as vigorously opposed to spiritual mingling as it is afraid of petrification, adjures us that, without surrendering either the church as an organism or the church as an institution, we must unite them both in the free church. The free church! *Free*, for the stream of Christian living must be able to flow unhindered, but let it continue to be *church*, for the stream will dissipate across the flat plains if its banks are demolished. "A free church"—there you see what can solve the riddle for us, for we must be *free* in order to escape Rome's paralysis, but no less must we be *church* in order to escape the draining away of our lifeblood as a result of spiritualism.

If Scripture is to be our touchstone here, and is to guide us in evaluating these voices, then it appears to me indubitable that only the last opinion is endorsed by Scripture. The first two perspectives that I outlined maintain the church either exclusively as an organism or exclusively as an institution. If either is the case, then the passage from the epistle to the Ephesians argues sufficiently against both pursuits, and argues for a free church that neither surrenders the organism of the church nor destroys the church as an institution.

"Rooted and grounded," says the apostle, and thereby declares with equal brevity and succinctness that twofold requirement, that double character trait of the Christian life. Rooted—that is the description of *organic* life; but also grounded—that is the requirement of the *institution*.

"Rooted" is the metaphor describing the free life that arises not through human artistry but immediately from the hand of the Creator, bearing in its own core the power of life and in its own seed the law of its life. You will find that metaphor earlier, in terms of the tree with spreading branches that grew from a mustard seed. It captures the spirit of what is termed "growing together into one plant," describing the bond that unites people with Christ. He is the vine, we are the branches, withering if we are separated from him but bearing fruit if we abide in him— this describes everything that lives organically, and does so with metaphors drawn from growing plants. Similarly, the yeast in those measures of meal points us to a fermentation process that

4

operates automatically. Surpassing every other figure, we have the metaphor of the body that Scripture prefers to use for the church, an image that requires organic life, a figure that binds the parts together by means of a power operating invisibly, one that refers to a natural growth occurring not through something added but through a force that comes to outward expression from the inside.

Rooted, to be sure, but also "grounded," for alongside that theme of fermentation and vital growth, another series of entirely different metaphors runs through Scripture, drawn not from *nature* but from *the work of human hands*. In that series, the metaphor of the church that we are given most frequently is not the growing body but the constructed *house*; a house consecrated by the Lord's Spirit to be his *temple*, and later expanding to the dimensions of an entire *city*, whose name will express its nature: "Jerusalem, that brings peace." The church not only grows, but is also *built*. This explains that repeated emphasis on the single *basis*, that repeated reference to the *foundation* on which the house must rest. Buttressed by its *pillars*, fastened together in its *security*, that house is held together by its outermost *cornerstone*. It rises upward, the *builders* rejoice, and the goal of everyone's effort is that the house may be *established*.

"Rooted and grounded" unites organism and institution, and where Scripture itself refuses to allow any separation, it weaves them together. By means of the person who sows and plants, the metaphor of vital growth overflows into that of the institution; by means of the living stone, the metaphor of the building flows over into that of the organism. The church of the Lord is one loaf, dough that rises according to its nature but nevertheless kneaded with human hands, and baked like bread. The church is called a multitude of priests, legitimated through birth but consecrated only through anointing. A bride brought forth by the Father but accepted by choice. A people, finally, that indeed sprouted from the living trunk but nevertheless organized with wisdom and guided with self-motivation.

That the text connects the two is not accidental but normative. Every viewpoint departs from Scripture that either dissolves the connection between both foundational themes, or while closely adhering to the one, erases the other. Every understanding of the church is to be considered mistaken that prevents the conjunction of these two or disparages one of these two.

2

The Church as Organism

INDEED, LET ME proceed, my friends! That law expressed by Paul's formulation applies not merely to the church but to every kind of life that comes into contact with human consciousness. "Eden is planted, but mankind will cultivate it." That is the fundamental law of creation. Which is to say: creation was fashioned by God, fashioned with life that surges and scintillates in its bosom, fashioned with the powers that lie dormant in its womb. Yet, lying there, it displayed but half its beauty. Now, however, God crowns it with humanity, who awakens its life, arouses its powers, and with human hands brings to light the glory that once lay locked in its depths but had not yet shone on its countenance.

The inanimate creation displays this. You need glance only at the terrain of our habitation and ask what it once was in its natural state and what it has become through the energetic activity of our ancestors. Similarly, witness the power that speeds our word along metal wires or our very persons along iron rails; this power lay embedded in that creation from the time of Eden already, but only now has it been discovered, analyzed, and harnessed by the spirit of man. Crops grow by organic power, but the human hand prepares a fertile soil for that crop, tames the wild acreage, prunes the wild shoots, guides the branches according to the flow of their juices, and by means of hybrids produces new kinds of plants. The wild forest creature surges and wriggles full of organic life, but only when tamed by people, bridled by the human hand, ennobled by human technique into thoroughbreds, does that wild natural power attain its goal. In short, compare the desolate place with the inhabited region, lay the creation *accompanied* by man alongside the creation *apart from* man, and everything bears witness, both of a creation immediately fashioned and of a perfecting of that creation that the Lord now completes *through man*.

But of course this is evident even more strongly in the world of mankind itself. One dimension of our humanity involves *instinctive* life; another involves our *conscious* life. Whatever operates instinctively in us comes automatically into being in and through us with an iron necessity. That is how the family comes about, as well as the life of society and the state, with the first stage of its development proceeding exclusively from natural impulse. For that reason it everywhere displays the same shape, follows the same law, is rooted in the same ground. But that is merely the first phase, the phase of bare organic life, displaying the features of a child—until finally it awakens in self-consciousness, analyzing the relationships belonging to that family, reflecting on that society, regulating that state by means of ideas, and ennobling organic life through the power of the institution.

Just as it was said in the creation story: ". . . his work which God created, to perfect it,"[1] that is how it is, my friends! Not as though to make a division, saying: "This is what the Lord wrought," and "This is what man made." If you insist on that contrast, then man is absolutely *nothing*, and would then be capable of *nothing*. I know of but One who called this mighty

---

1   These words appear in Genesis 2:3, as found in the *Statenvertaling* of 1637.

system into being, and now directs and propels all its parts. That is the Lord! He is also the One who does this with the second creation, using us as instruments, so that later, if we refuse to be converted to him, in his sovereignty he casts us out. Whatever we endeavor—the plan we follow, the strength we apply, the material we employ, the basis upon which we build—all of it is his. We ourselves who do it, what are we other than flimsy creatures? For that reason, even with that distinction as well, he alone is the Cause, the Source, the Fountainhead, and the Worker of whatever is built or is grown, of whatever is grounded or rooted. Everything is from and through and unto him!

Had there been no sin, with these comments everything would have been said regarding the church—assuming that apart from sin there still would have been a church on earth, something we deny.

Meanwhile, the fact of sin lies in our path, sin with its regrettable aftermath of corrupting souls, disrupting joy, and causing this earth to be cursed. Sin turned this mighty system in its course by shifting it off its axis anchored in the Eternal, and due to sin there is no longer any consummation of the powers for this creation.

Had sin not come, Eden would have been cultivated, creation would gradually have been perfected, until finally it would have joined together with the life of heaven and transitioned into eternal glory. But now that is no longer the case. The vital root has been severed, the foundation wrested from its moorings. Whatever may be growing from that cancerous root, whatever may be constructed on that shattered foundation, it continues to bear the mark of its origin, and thus never reaches to the height of heaven. Though developments leap forward with giant steps, though every age brings to light for us a new treasure of powers, that blossoming fruit can never swell to its full greatness, but falls down from the branch, prematurely ripened and inwardly cancerous, having displayed only a false blossom. That is what is meant by "this heaven and this earth shall pass away." The relationship is irreparably broken. This sinful life cannot overflow into eternal life.

And yet this creation will not be lost—but only its shell will one day be cast aside and a new form will emerge from it, developed from a life germ that was laid within creation *after* the Fall. The cosmic conflagration is coming, but from this cosmic conflagration the precious metal will be saved into which a higher power will transform a part of its life. So although this world, even in its boldest development, will never reach the heights of heaven, nevertheless a glorious life will germinate from this world, a life whose seed descended from heaven, a life that one day will be melded together with this heaven in immaculate radiance.

That life, which exists in Christ as *human* life, that is, as life that in the highest sense functioned for this creation, proceeds from grace and not from sin-affected nature. That life is a miracle. It does not arise from this earth, but breaks in upon the earth. This life penetrates into the world's joints, melts down whatever it finds, and transforms it into its own life. Though compatible with this earth as the earth existed before sin, it is exactly for that reason in fierce opposition against this earth as it has become through sin. Not merely in degree, but in kind; not merely in form, but in principle—you need only behold the cross!—separated from sinful life, it can never grow alongside that life from the same root, it can never be constructed alongside that life on the same foundation.

A double stream flows today through the kingdom of spirits. The stream of the old life that propels its waves onward but yet silts up before it reaches the ocean. And within that, a different stream, one that has trickled down from God's holy mountain, which never loses its course though it appears to merge with those other waters, and which, soon turning aside, carves out its own bed as it proceeds toward the ocean. Neither the organism nor the institution of this old life is adequate for that new life. That new life flows from another source and before long forms its own boundaries. As unique life, it must be rooted in itself; because it is a unique life, it must create a unique form in an independent institution.

That organism and that institution is the church. For anyone who denies miracles, for anyone who acknowledges only the creation of nature, that church has no meaning and can offer no lodging. That demand must be pressed very sharply in all its rigor. It comes down to the difference of degree and of kind between sinful life and sacred life.

"Consecrated and unconsecrated" or "everything alike," that is the question that either inflames our love for the church or dampens it, and that must determine her right of existence. But once that separation is a reality for us, and thus a church is required by our faith, then it is obvious that such a church must obey her law of life, namely, that she needs both an organism and an institution.

The church is an organism because she bears a unique life within herself and self-consciously upholds the independence of that life over against the old life. The church is an organism because she lives according to her own rule and must follow her own vital law. The church is an organism, finally, because what will later unfold from her buds is fully supplied already within her seed.

As our fathers so correctly put it, the church is rooted in eternal election, or as the apostle expresses it here, she is rooted in *love*. Rooted in another soil, therefore, than what the field of this world offers. If *selfishness* dominates there, then love is the indestructible material with which the eternal is dispersed. And precisely in that eternal field the organism of the church sends forth its roots, from that eternal it draws its life juices, under the rays of that eternal it flourishes.

That organism is the heart of the church. From that heart her lifeblood flows, and where that pulse of her life ceases, the institution alone never constitutes the church. If you send missionaries out to remote places, if they do not bring with them this vital seed, your church is never born in yonder places. A church cannot be manufactured; a polity, no matter how tidy, and a confession, no matter how spotless, are powerless to form a church if the living organism is absent. Let those who intentionally deny that unique life of the church just try to imitate the church of Christ in their own locale, and people will see once again what has been seen so often already: with the erosion of the soil their building collapses.

3

The Church as Institution

A N ORGANISM, YES—but here as well, the coming to life is followed by consciousness, and with that conscious life there is a second creation as the advancement, nurture, and unfolding of what the organism carries within itself. So in addition to the *growth* there is a *building*, a *plant* but also an *organization*, a *root* but also a *basis* beneath it—an organism but also an institution.

The church did not possess this when she first arose. At that point her life was more instinctive, since the fullness of that life was not yet analyzed, the demand of that life not yet articulated, and its appearance in the world still tarried. And still, already at that point the apostles appeared to inject that young plant with an organization. They arrange, they regulate, they include and exclude, and they seek to give a form to this life that would preserve it from dissipating. This demonstrates the need of an institution, even though to her own hurt, the church had virtually neglected this building of the institution for a century; so much so that the scourge of Gnosticism had to overtake her first, and the self-consumption of Donatism had to gnaw at her life, before she understood her duty of returning to the apostolic trail.

The church cannot lack the institution, for the very reason that all life among human beings needs analysis and arrangement. This is how it is with the soul, this is how it is with the body, which lives organically but even so, it languishes if no regulating consciousness guides it and no structuring hand provides for it. This is how it goes with justice, which does indeed grow among humanity but even so, it must be classified, described, and maintained, and exists among no nation apart from a judicial institution. It is the same with God's revelation that became organic and still could not dispense with the institution of Israel or the form of document and writing. Indeed, it is this way above all with Christ himself, whose life does not simply flow about aimlessly but is manifested in human particularity through the incarnation.

This applies as well to the church. Since Christianity does not animate merely an individual, but binds many together, there necessarily comes into existence a legal relationship that degenerates into confusion if there are no judicial rules. Since it places a task not simply on the individual but also on all believers together, there must be an organization that regulates the mandate for everything that happens in the name of everyone. Finally, since its own life constantly threatens to dissipate into the life of the world, it must not merely allow a spiritual sorting to function at the depth but also allow a tangible authentication to function at the surface, which determines inclusion and exclusion.

But this is still merely the institution from its human side, my friends, which recedes entirely in the face of the much more serious significance that the institution of the church possesses as God's institution. In this sense it manifests not merely the organism, but the institution is a means supplied by God for feeding and expanding that organism. For just as was the case after the initial creation, here too there is a further bringing to life through man as instrument.

For behold, on Pentecost the Holy Spirit descends, I do not say, without preparation, but still immediately, and he creates the church among men who could never have brought it forth. But after that miraculous creation, things were different. From now on, it is the church herself through which the Holy Spirit, who dwells within her, expands and unfolds that church. From now on, there is mutual interpenetration, a reciprocal influence. *From the organism the institution is born, but also through the institution the organism is fed.*

"Go, teach all nations and baptize them." "Teach and baptize," says the founding document of that institution. "Word and Sacrament"—behold the foundational parameters of the design according to which the institution is constructed. For neither the proclamation of that Word nor the administration of that sacrament is an organic operation. They presuppose human consciousness; they need human organization; they require a human act. They do not operate automatically, but through man as the instrument of the Lord. Their figurative representation is not that of something growing from a root, but of something being constructed on a foundation.

It is a mistake to view the church simply as an association of like-minded people, one that simply manifests what they share. The church is not the organ of humanity, but humanity is born from her maternal womb, as her organ. The church exists before humanity, for the church gives birth to humanity. The church stands above humanity, for the church nurtures humanity. "She is a mother"—to use Calvin's beautiful expression—"whose womb not only carried us, whose breast not only nursed us, but whose tender care leads us to the goal of faith. . . . Those to whom he is a Father, the Church must also be Mother, and apart from her motherly care no one grows to maturity."[1] The church is our mother! Behold the beautiful image, my friends, that expresses so attractively both the organism and the institution. Her womb granted us life, her care nurtures us.

---

1 Cf. John Calvin, *Institutes of the Christian Religion*, ed. John T. McNeill, Library of Christian Classics, vols. 20-21 (Philadelphia: Westminster Press, 1960), 4.1.1 and 4.1.4; Kuyper seems to be quoting from memory.

But it is precisely this "nurturing" that renders the institution absolutely indispensable. Where every child starts from scratch, makes his own way, and is left to himself, there we find no hint of nurture. To nurture means specifically to bring to the child the treasure that was acquired thus far, leading everyone along the pathway already cleared. The essence of nurture is to unleash, to feed, and to prune fully organic life, according to a fixed protocol chosen purposefully, according to an unswerving principle that governs the entire context. So there is no nurture where there is no regularity, no nursery where there is no order. Every sphere of nurture involves organism and institution.

Certainly, the Spirit of God is a fountain of water within the human heart, springing forth unto eternal life. But the water coming from that source within the heart discharges into a *stream* that incorporates the advances made by every new generation, offers its waters to each coming generation, propelling its ripples further and deeper in order that, as it irrigates every generation, it may connect them with each other. The organism of the church is the nourishing source for that stream, but the institution is the bed that carries its current, the banks that border its waters. Only in this way is there development, only in this way is the progress of the Christian life conceivable. It is the church that makes us stand upon the shoulders of those who went before us, and preserves our harvest for the generation that comes after us.

Only through the institution can the church offer us that unique life sphere where the ground we tread, the air we breathe, the language we speak, and the nourishment of our spirit are not those of the world but of the Holy Spirit. That institution positions itself between us and the world, in order to protect the uniqueness of our life with the power supplied by that unanimity and that order. Through that institution, with all its procedures and groupings and rich ramifications, the fruit—the higher nature of the new life—must be displayed to us as a fixed form in reality. The consciousness of the life of the heart cannot be awakened anywhere but in such a sympathetic atmosphere, and only the institution offers us such a life sphere in more than a vague sense.

For that reason we have such an institution that is itself thoroughly formed, that works formatively upon the individual, structurally upon the family, directively upon society, and that chooses the Christian school as her vestibule. An institution that calls into being, from the root of its own life, a unique science and art, that strives in its confession for a more correct expression of the eternal truth and for an ever purer worship of the Holy One. An institution, finally, that preserves discipline and justice, and is nevertheless flexible, tender, and supple, adapting to the nature of each, accommodating itself to every nation, and in every age adopting the language of its time—behold what the church of Christ needs as desperately as she needs her rootedness in God.

Let people simply ensure that the root of the organism continues to be in harmony with the foundation, and let people never separate the building of the church from her growth and inception. Let people continually draw from the organism their motive power, their formative capacity, and beware of Rome's error that moves in precisely the opposite direction, as Rome wishes to govern the growth according to the building, and contrary to the nature of every kind of life, allows the "rooted" to follow only when the "grounded" has first been completed.

"*First* rooted, *then* grounded, but both bound *together* at their most inner core!" Let that be the slogan of the church living from God's Word. May the sovereign election of God's eternal counsel remain for those who are the Dutch Reformed Church, according to the language of our fathers, the *cor ecclesiae*, the heart of the church, and thus the root from which she blossoms, but also the firm foundation upon which her building must be built. The organism is the essence, the institution is the form. To say it once again with Calvin: "What God has joined together, you, O man, may not put asunder!" [*Institutes*, 4.1.1].

———— ✧ ————

Finally, if someone asks whether the building known as the visible church would be the completion of the spiritual temple building, such that the visible church on earth should be identified with the kingdom of God, I would counter with this question: does the prolonged tragedy of the church on earth tolerate for a moment the fueling of this delusion?

No, my friends, it is an entirely different bond that binds together church and kingdom of God. I prefer to indicate this for you in terms of an analogy. You know that in our cities we often see a stack of wood on an open lot. Bricks are piled up, joists are brought in, people walk around with measuring tools and plumbs; on that lot a wooden frame is raised, tied together with poles and boards and cross-beams, looking more misshapen than elegant. That scaffolding, as people call it, appears to be constantly rising higher, its dimensions constantly corresponding to the outline of the building. But that wooden frame is not the actual enclosure, that scaffolding lashed together is not the wall of the house. For look, when after many days the cornice is brought in and the gables are anchored in place, then that scaffolding is torn down, that frame is dismantled, and the house that was skillfully constructed out of sight now sparkles in the grandeur of its lines and shimmers in the beauty of its form before the eyes of everyone.

By now you understand what I am saying, my friends! That scaffolding is the church on earth—as she appears at present to the eye: defective and misshapen. It must remain for a time, for who can build without scaffolding? But one day, when the cornice is brought in and the last stone is set, then that scaffolding will be removed, then that church on earth will fall away, and then that glorious temple will shimmer in its eternal beauty— a temple that hitherto had not existed, but that the builders had been building while supported by that church.

4

The Struggle within the Church To Be Both Rooted and Grounded

SO THEN, MY friends, in the apostolic word we have found a clearly delineated starting point, and together with me you sense that this decides the criticism about the currents in our ecclesiastical life and the judgment about the state of our church. Precisely through the separation of organism and institution, and the indispensability of both, that judgment arises automatically.

In that connection, if my eye automatically focuses first on the modernist current, then I am not asking that someone praise my courage because I oppose it. That courage is completely imaginary in a situation that tolerates no contradiction. If I speak this way, it is merely because clarity about the situation is indispensable, and silence merely fuels misunderstanding.

The church of Christ—this appeared clear to us just now—lives from a *unique* organism and needs a *unique* institution on account of sin. Leave sin out of consideration, and the church becomes inconceivable, since the world itself would then be the church. When considering the question whether a church has a right to exist, everything depends on that other question: what do we think about sin? If we view it as absolute, then there has to be a church; if for us sin is merely relative, then there is no place for a church. If creational life has become genuinely impotent through sin and profaned in the deepest sense, then—but only then—purity of life is imaginable as something coming down into that creation, breaking in as by a miracle, and thus blossoming from its own root that differs in its life-law and life-principle from the root of the world.

By contrast, if people refer to that conclusion, as I read recently in the devotional publications from that camp, as "deceiving each other with drivel" when emphasizing the depravity of our nature and arguing on the basis of human impotence that one can accomplish not even the smallest beginning of obedience—then, as everyone senses, it is merely through lack of consistency that such people keep using the name of church. If people think that the life of Christ does not differ absolutely from sinful life and so baptize their spirit in the waters of sacrilege in order to erase the boundary line that separates the consecrated domain from the profane domain—if they refer to those as a *club* who, with Jesus, talk about "many who are called, but few are chosen"—then it brooks no contradiction to claim that in that case a church as a unique organism is unthinkable and necessarily merges together with society. Or if you will, if people view miracles not as indispensable but as impossible, and if they reject every fracture that would disturb the grand process of things, then there can be no other life than life from the world itself, and a church that is from the world would be a self-contradictory notion.

Consequently, my conviction rests on this basis, that the modernist current has no moral right to exist in our church, even though it can still maintain its judicial right on the basis of a law-book, such as we have, that eschews nothing so much as the proper administration of justice.

The proposal that despite contradictory principles, we should nevertheless live together in the same house is therefore not acceptable, because for people to be called brothers and sisters they must have come forth from the same womb, and the art is still awaiting discovery whereby one can make the same kind of plant grow from two kinds of roots.

Finally, if people are seeking to maintain the church as an association for spreading moral and religious life, a nursery of piety, even then that demand must be denied them, and I do not hesitate to adopt Luther's bold proverb: "The purpose of the church is not to make people pious but Christian. One can be pious and still not Christian. A true Christian knows nothing of his own piety."

That unique organism, denied by the modernists, as you know, is gloriously maintained by that other movement that I prefer to call by the name "irenic." "Irenic, peace-loving"—not as though they would not love to fight for their own slogan. For everyone who has a principle fights for it unto death. But "irenic, peace-loving," because they still consider a solution possible that avoids the pain of irreparable break. Do not think, however, that such people lack a deep view of sin. On the contrary. For them the cleft is very deep that separates the holy and consecrated life from the unconsecrated. In fighting for a unique life that Christianity shares with none other, they have rather gone ahead of others and have acquired unfading laurels. For them the Christian life is *rooted* very firmly. Indeed, they do not merely affirm this initial term of the apostolic watchword, but rather they are precisely the ones who once again have raised from the dead that grand conception of a unique life, that rich principle of a unique organism, to make it live again in the consciousness of the church.

But even as every struggle that must once again give voice to a forgotten word, even as every movement that comes to restore the disrupted balance, is automatically inclined to throw all its weight onto one side of the scale and thereby itself to lapse into imbalance, so too it has happened in this movement. Because the church has forgotten the component of being *rooted*, the "irenics" are forgetting the component of being *grounded*. This explains why this side is weak in terms of the church question, and continues to lack a concept of the church with which it can implement its sharp contrast of "sacred and profane." This is like what happens with anyone who dares not build for himself; unfortunately, he must live in what others have built, and gradually that domicile wins his affection; in spite of himself he protects it to the end, and the solemn duty to build for himself gradually retreats into the depths of his conscience.

If such a movement arises in a time like ours, when especially the church question dominates every other issue, then, naturally, the waste of energy entailed by such a tortured position cannot remain hidden, and either they must advance from being rooted to being grounded, or else, without knowing it themselves, they will retreat even from being rooted.

Their favorite position—that the Christian life, no matter how intermingled it may be with foreign life in Jesus' church, nevertheless through its own power will arrest, convert, and control that foreign element—seeks mistakenly to apply to the church what in the great battlefields of the world is contested by no one. Most assuredly, the God who is with us will show himself mightier in this battle than the spirit fighting against us, as long as we do not resist God's ordinance that he desires to display that spiritual power through and in his church. The marketplace of the world, not the church, is the arena where we wrestle for the prize, the racetrack where we wage the contest for the wreath. Far from being that battlefield itself, the church is rather like the army tent of the Lord where soldiers strengthen themselves before that battle, where they treat their wounds after the battle, and where one who has become "prisoner by the sword of the Word" is fed at the table of the Lord. That unsustainable striving for wanting only to be rooted, to be only an organism—what else is that but a return to the embryonic life even before the senses of the church came into use and before her feet were firmly planted. No, my friends, what was valid for the early church cannot be valid for our time, because it fails to appreciate the church's growth.

At the same time, the other extreme of the apostolic word cannot exist alone either. Those people committed to externality, who seek a sound and well-built house at any price but show no sign of concern for the life lived inside the house—those people infatuated with the surface of things, who delight in looking into a clear mirror but never bother themselves about what is dying off in the hidden recesses—they can never build the church, because the church of Christ never permits her walls to be constructed with dead stones. O, go ahead and cut off all those in the church of the fathers who cannot boast of having blood "free of foreign stains." Measure everything in your church down to the last mark on your flawless yardstick. Bring your confession once again to unchallenged domination in your church. Indeed, let the external shape of your church be raised along the purest lines so that the church of every nation may be aroused to jealousy, and display a church so unblemished and unwrinkled as has never been seen in the course of time. . . . Even then, no matter how radiantly that house may glisten with its architecturally beautiful lines, your church may not bear the name of Christ if you banish life from her out of fear that people might tarnish your sheen, and if you exclude God's Spirit out of fear that his mighty works may tear up your beautiful pavement. Such a church, O my, what else would she be other than a rich Lazarus, yet where both physician and medicine are absent, and who will carry his sick ones there? No, beloved! Being "grounded," being "founded," cannot benefit you if you do not also have a life that blossoms forth from the eternal root.

Finally, there is one last current, or let me rather say, above Jesus' church there hovers a misting cloud that, bursting forth, now here and then there, continually makes the sounds of little rivulets but whose characteristic feature is that they never merge into one stream. You recognize that effort. Where, I ask, do you not detect its busy hands, in which field do you not find its footprints? O, I do love it, that zeal to convert that spares no one but seizes everyone and surmounts every obstacle, to lead souls to Christ.

And yet, I may not deny that there is something in this restless drive that disturbs me. Conversion is pressed, but instruction of the converted must be postponed—how could it be otherwise?—there is no time, for eyes and hearts are already focused on making more new converts. People rejoice especially in the number of converts. So they think they can dispense with any test and they welcome with nebulous indeterminacy every person as an ally who, on whatever basis, along whatever path, from whatever motive, simply wants to march in our ranks and join us in talking about the Lord, as though prevenient grace has stopped working, covenant blessing has lost its power, the church's past is purposeless, and every conversion, beyond the influence of God's faithful covenant, is an isolated fact, an incidental work of the Lord's Spirit. Sometimes it appears as though God's elect are not generated through rebirth from the one Christ in shared parentage, but are plucked from the river like drowning victims by the arm of the Spirit.

That may not remain unchallenged, beloved! Spiritual revival is an extraordinary grace, I know, sometimes the only saving means, but when it is made the rule it subverts Jesus' church. Then it is nothing but cuttings planted together here and there in beds, but then there is no root, and the vine has no stem that binds the branches into a unity. "Together with all the saints," says the man from Tarsus in the verse following our text, and that connection is never neglected without very serious injury. For the bitter fruit is already manifested. We already see how each one wants to travel under his own flag, to privateer under his own ensign. Already the many-headed monster of that all-fracturing individualism is sticking out its horns. O, if people only realized that in this way bricks are indeed brought in and piled up, but that pile of bricks cannot stack itself up into a wall. Without design, cement, and builder, a house will never emerge from those stones.

5

A Call for Freedom
To Be the Church

BUT EVEN THOUGH I oppose those three previous movements, my friends, I hasten to add that each finds its cause and thus its incontestable right of existence in the untenable church situation in which we live. Our house is not right. We must *rebuild or relocate*. Everyone is saying so. If any are not, you can be sure it is fear for the feverish tension of the crisis, far more than calm tranquility, that makes them say so. If a deep sleep were to fall on everyone and in our dreams the crisis, as if by magic, were ended and the purge had come, each of us would want to hold on to that dream when waking up to reality. People fear not the fruit, but the pain, of the crisis. People sense that this way would lead to improvement, but they shrink back from what must happen first.

I dare to pronounce that judgment, my friends, for I see that it is so. Every conversation with leaders of the most divergent movements convinces me time and again that these same people who amid the clamor of voices want to ward off the crisis, nevertheless in private, in the inner recesses of their heart, are busy with new building plans. And it is only because they cannot have "the fruit of the crisis apart from the crisis" that they are held back from completing their design.

How else could it be, my friends? For both from this side as from the other side, we know without a doubt—every beat of our heart tells us, we sense it in our innards—that we have become altogether different spirits. If that is so, then I pray you, what can living together yield other than concealment of principle or interminable conflict? Therefore, I ask you, not in the name of Christ—for I do not know whether you would all understand that as I intend it—but appealing to your moral earnestness that clings to what you all call sacred for your own heart—indeed, with my hand reaching into your conscience—I ask you: is any more tragic spectacle imaginable than a church of Christ that either dooms people to *lying* or condemns them to *fraternal war*? Either *silencing* what is sacred to us, or *devouring* one another—may that be the choice for Jesus' church who before all else is called to uproot the lie and allay bitterness?

Should you reply: Then let the church be simply a nursery for piety and for moral living—then I would still ask: Can there be inner piety as long as on both sides, heads are so hot and hearts so disquieted, and the fiercest partisanship sweeps everyone away with its current? Instead, immorality is nourished by a church that leaves her sacrifice unconsecrated at the foot of her altar, and tempts even her own priests to a breach of faith.

Even so, people say that the church question has been inflated by merely a few individuals. No, my friends; rather, it lies there thrown in our path by God; it lies there as a stone of stumbling that will expose hearts. O, how much more free would our conscience be, how much more tender our praying, how much more persistent our fellowship with God, if we were finished once and for all with that dancing on a tightrope in order to preserve the balance, if once and for all we could steer clear of the Scylla of lies and the Charybdis of false peace. We call for *peace* but also for *truth*, for *truth* but also for *peace*. Therefore our watchword is: Purge the situation, because that purging alone will once again "wed truth to peace."

To that end we demand nothing else than freedom. Freedom, because no organism flourishes unless it can spread its roots freely and unfurl its crown of leaves in the fresh air. Freedom, so that the organism of our church herself may show us her nature, spell out for us her law of living, and form the life sphere needed for her blossoming. Freedom, so that in that system every force may discover its course, every gear its axis, every part its proper limits. Freedom, finally, so that—with petty obstructionism gone—the battle may once again become spiritual, a face-to-face encounter of opposing sides, with no pedantic standard but the life-law itself choosing what element the church can still assimilate within her own life, and what she must reject out of hand as toxic for her spirit and dangerous for her life.

For that, the requirement of liberation is threefold. Let the church be free from the state, free from the money purse, and free from the pressure of office.

Let the church be free from the state, and thereby correct the enormous mistake committed by Jesus' church fourteen centuries ago to curry the emperor's favor. For precisely because the church wanted to dominate, she did not dominate the nations, and only if she is willing once again to serve will she win back her dominion. As long as a crown adorned her brow, the church was the "do-nothing queen," "princess without influence," and the mighty state, no matter how much it appeared to be her servant, was in truth her master. But even though this is how the church lost her freedom, even though the state itself subsequently took the crown, the church's freedom is still her inalienable right. No sovereign prince can ever break the sovereign right of the church's anointed King. Here there is no obsolescence, here there is no acquiescence. Because the church is an organism, the church possesses her unique life and thus her unique principle of law [rechtsbeginsel]. Therefore, whoever seeks to force the operation of our church law to conform to the requirements of civil law or the workings of public law is confusing what in principle is distinct, and is surrendering the freedom and independence of the church organism.

Next, let the church be free from money. It does not suit the church of Christ to let herself be bound by golden fetters or silver chains to what conflicts with her nature. The early church began with nothing else than the Holy Spirit, and still the church's treasure gradually grew into a gold mine. People have since then plundered it, and the Lord tolerated that theft so that his church would demonstrate what she treasured as of greater value, namely: the faith that had landed the gold in her lap, or the gold that faith had obtained for her. "With me," says the Lord, "gold and silver consist of enduring good and righteousness." But the state in turn declares: "With me you find the millions, with me you find the money that is needed for your church!" It is true, the church needs money. Now then, two offers are being directed to you. Whose promise will you trust, O church? The promise of him who provides you the gold as the fruit of faith, or the promise of the state who binds you with its gold as with chains, in order to cause the freedom of faith to stumble in its course? The choice is yours, but this I tell you: your faith treasury must become increasingly more depleted as long as you do not learn to hate the money that is not free. The adage applies here as well: whoever would be saved will lose. Only one who is able to be poor becomes rich. Only one who dares disdain the gold has discovered the goldmine.

Finally, the church must become free from the pressure of the office, the pressing burden of one of the ministries. The beautiful words spoken by the one who installed me—"that for the teacher-pastor, the church is not only the field white unto harvest, but simultaneously an immeasurable multitude of fellow priests"—unleashed a hallelujah in the depths of my heart, and my soul prayed for a blessed Amen that might arise from the powerful activity of the church in response to those eloquent words. The office of pastor-teacher, as it has developed during the course of the present century as a result of idle overseers and a lethargic church, would be well suited in a church that could be only an institution, but it is completely out of place in the church of the Lord that, as a living organism, is herself consecrated to the ministry of the altar. One who holds office must be rooted in the priesthood of the church. Apart from that intimate relationship, the office becomes domineering.

6

A Call To Defend
the Reformed Church
As Organism and Institution

PERHAPS YOU ARE asking: how then are we to achieve such liberation? My friends, the Lord is our General in this battle, and the victory beckons us if we are but willing to follow him. Not we, but he creates the opportunity; he paves the routes; his are the preparations. Whoever does not find rest in that is not fighting for the Lord.

Let us only press forward and further into every domain that he opens for us, into every fortress to which he grants us access. The pretentious bond of unreformed church government will ultimately snap if we but adopt the watchword that comes with autonomy, that is to say: the "self-government and self-direction of the congregation." That is *our* form of church life. That alone is Reformed. Within Rome's organization, each congregation is merely an impassive member that is never energized by its own impulse but always by the now infallible head.[1] In Lutheran

---

1 Only a month earlier, on 18 July 1870, the First Vatican Council had declared the pope infallible in matters of faith and morals.

countries the life bonds of the congregations are consolidated in the hands of the state. In both systems the church exists first, only thereafter to give birth to the congregations. But that is not how it went on Reformed soil. There the congregations existed first, there the great stream of the church was not brought forth until the flowing together of the congregations, there the strictly administrative church government rose up from the independent congregations.

But do not forget that a Reformed form of church life grows up only in a church that is Reformed in her heart. Ours cannot be a colorless Christianity, one that differs in degree but not in kind from a version of Christianity that transcends faith divisions. Each person's calling is not merely to be a human being but to have one's own character. So too here, to be not merely a congregation but a congregation with its own hallmark is an inexorable demand for the church in every place.

People are well aware of what has become of the Great Protestant movement.[2] How ignominiously it has melted away! How to her disgrace Rome's power has again burst forth, virtually at its greatest precisely in the financial area, where it had wanted to engage the battle with Rome.

O, I fully agree that anyone entering a house in ordinary times is not thinking about the foundation on which it rests; and so also in Jesus' church there can be times when people dwell together and labor together, hardly bothering themselves about any principles. But in times like those we are now experiencing, now when in every area the foundations are being undermined, now when everything is pressing down to the depths and people are proceeding restlessly to pry the deepest principles loose, now in these times it would be all too naïve, all too negligent, for people to sidestep the issue of principles any longer. No, in times of peace let the sword remain unsharpened, but when the order to advance sounds through the ranks, one must not blunt

---

2 Kuyper is here referring to the no-popery movement organized in April 1853.

the sharpness of its edge. If people have without injury permitted the sharpness of our principles to become dull over time, now that the time for self-defense has arrived the sword must be wielded once again or we will stand powerless in battle.

Therefore our church must again become not merely Christian, not merely Protestant, but Reformed: God is her Sovereign, eternal election is the heart blood of her life, and God's Word the foundation that cannot be dislodged, upon which she stands with both her feet.

Lastly, by appreciating the Reformed contours of church life, we are not closing off any development of our ecclesiastical organization. The Reformed ecclesiastical principle contains the germ of a rich, multi-dimensional development of which until now only the first new growth has budded. Let that which has come about in the absence of a proper church now become joined with her. Let her school, which in former times was lost through her own fault, be recaptured in the spiritual vitality of faith with the devotion of every effort. The collection of associations that have come into existence in the voluntary sector must be brought into relationship with her, in order by means of unity and order to double every effort. Development must occur in our confession, development in our worship, development in our ecclesiastical government, development in all of the activities of the congregation. Above all, let our church not ignore the great social issues of "promiscuity and overpopulation," of "labor and pauperism." The church especially must battle against sin; especially the church has the calling to support the relative right of the lower class over against the spirit of the times. Let whatever is oppressed have the church's support: may the poor find the church to be a place of refuge, and may the church become for rich and poor together once again an Angel of peace who gently leads us from both the abuses and the utopias of our age back to the ordinance of God's Word.

My friends, let me summarize. If our church is currently presenting us with two entangled shrubs, fastened with triple bonds and thereby hindered in her growth—those bonds must be burst—that is the liberation. From the very root, up the stem, those shrubs must be disentangled—this is the implementation of the principles. Once liberated, the real shrub must grow new blossoms—that is the development to which God himself is calling us.

7

Closing Exhortations

CONGREGATION OF AMSTERDAM! Your calling in this regard needs no coaching. The importance of the very size of your congregation indicates your obligation. You have already done much; your struggle has already been glorious. O, what beautiful days await you! For of this I am certain: a congregation that a half-century ago defended her independent government with such manliness,[1] yes, even more, that once sat at Da Costa's feet, brooks no comparison and, until the goal is achieved, will not lay down her sword.

"Not many noble, not many influential"—perhaps those royal words apply to you as well. O, may you be but noble in heart, may you be but influential in the kingdom of God, then hope beckons us with a laugh of joyous ecstasy. Those among

---

1 In 1815, Classis Amsterdam, at the urging of the pastors from the Amsterdam church, was the only body that lodged an official protest against the reorganization of the governance of the Reformed Church by the government that effectively placed the denomination under the control of the government's Ministry of Worship.

you who have received the truth of God from the hands of your ancestors, may you reach for nothing but the "Word." Let that Word hold sway with power in your own heart, let it hold sway with majesty around your hearth, let it govern life with its purifying influence in all of life, let each one contribute but a single drop of the water of life, and O . . . I think I already hear it cascading down, that irresistible mountain stream that will flow from such small droplets down Israel's bluffs.

People had placed the sedative to your lips and you had almost died, O church of our fathers! But God revived your spirit, your heart is beating once again, your blood is coursing through the veins again, your limbs are already moving. O, continue to awaken and rise from your dishonored bed. You have only to lift high your crowned head and the former inheritance is yours.

Permit me, congregation, to join your ranks in that contest. Not in order to hasten hotheadly along paths that our eye has never surveyed. That person misses the target who with one shot seeks to achieve what requires years of effort. No, but in order to keep battling with calm patience, quiet confidence, and persistent energy while the prayer never vanishes from our lips: "Lord! Guide me onto that rock that is too high for my strength."

I offer you my heart and my hand. I pray only this: do not demand that I ever lend my hand to an external building that lacks the inner rootedness of the heart. As minister of the Word, I have to preach that Word to you, and my strength lies in that alone. What you recently sang to me: "Do not conceal from us what has been commanded to you, for the congregation is listening," I will in God's strength accomplish, even if I have to flog you in your conscience, even if people will leave because of the harshness of my words.

Indeed, permit me to conclude, congregation, by declaring that what I am pursuing is not simply the restoration of the church; what I intend is not simply doing battle with whomever dislikes my efforts. No. What moves my soul, what I beseech from my God, is that he may grant me to shine before your eye a single ray of light from that eternally rich, never exhaustively adored, mercy that is in Christ Jesus. What arouses my zeal is simply this, that I may dip the tips of my fingers in that Fountain of eternal Love, in order to lay a few drops of those cool waters of grace on the burning lips of your heart. And if I then also seek the restoration of the church, if I then also reach for the sword—it is only because, congregation, I am convinced that the minister of Christ may not sit idly by while the access to those waters of life is barricaded for the Lord's congregation.

I will direct an additional word to those, congregation, who are clothed with honor in your midst.

You are the first who honored me, Gentlemen, who as guardians and caregivers have been entrusted with the government of our church. You have already heard what it was from your past that aroused my admiration, how I applaud your courage in standing up when a half-century ago the congregation's freedom was endangered by governmental whimsy. The congregation has thanked you for that manly posture when recently they extended their confidence to you and chose to be freely governed by you instead of submitting to outside interference. May that proud spirit continue to animate you, may that freedom bear its generous fruit through your administration, and may the congregation demonstrate, by supporting you energetically, that they appreciate their independence as well as your care.

Maintain that independence also in the domain assigned to you, you members of the consistory and leaders of the congregation, you who especially in these perilous days bear such precious responsibility. Experience has already taught me what it frequently costs to defend the right of the congregation against the power of the church. Nevertheless I appeal to you: do not shrink back. Do not falter in this battle. You are from the congregation. From her you received your mandate. She is looking to you. Carry on with our ancient Reformed life, then, with good courage; carry it on in new forms, and as overseers and caretakers of the poor enjoy the same rights and the same rank with your pastors; but then join them also in contributing in equal measure to the work of ministry, each in his own field of activity. Above all, let us not focus on externals. Building up the congregation spiritually, feeding her with the Word of the Lord, remains our first calling in every battle. May our passionate zeal make us faithful especially in that!

To you, my fellow office-bearers, let me extend my thanks for the friendly goodwill with which you have received me. O, how I would wish I could say to you all: "Brothers, accept this young man in your hallowed circle so that hand in hand with you I may serve the one Lord." If regrettably I cannot say this to everybody, may it then apply at the very least to those of you who still stand fast in the Word and with me cling firmly to the Christ of God in quiet faith. And you who think you must not do this, who out of deep conviction fight against what for me is more sacred than anything else, O, I know that you would despise me if from my position, playing with what is holy, I sought to cover over the chasm that yawns so widely between us. Therefore I ask only this from you: let our association be uncomplicated, our relationship genuine, and may gallant openness and candid speech characterize the battle that you have undertaken with the church, and therefore the church has undertaken with you. Let us not conceal from each other, either here or in our daily interaction, the most serious rupture that, if things continue as they are, will turn out to be irreparable from both sides. And since faith separates us, accept from my side the sincere declaration that precisely because of that rupture, I sense my calling all the more to minister to you as much as lies within me, in the quest for mutual service as we strive to be of help to one another.

Finally, a word of thanks to you, my brother, who introduced me to the congregation three days ago. Your warmth of language cheered my heart. What you said was what you yourself had experienced, and every heart sensed it: that fire that came through in your words was not artificially ignited. While you once picked up the pen in order to contend against my efforts,[2] I feel the need to tell the congregation how much I appreciate your efforts. I wanted to be presented to the congregation particularly by you, so that it would be evident how little my heart is closed to being contradicted and how highly I value a fraternal judgment. Continue, brother, with the bonds of grace, to bring back what has drifted away, to seek the lost, according to the talents so richly bestowed upon you. And if not everyone can follow you with that creative power, with that ceaseless persistence, "to seek the lost" remains the endeavor of us all, the one for that individual sheep, the other for the lost sheepfold.

And now, congregation, I conclude with one more request for you. I left many people behind, but nevertheless I am coming to you with an open heart. Do not withhold from me the love that my heart needs and that provides such powerful support. Only, let it be a love rooted in a decisive choice, grounded in love for God's Word. Do not forsake me, but serve me with your fraternal judgment, and may what binds us together be not craven reciprocal blandishments, but the very serious discipline of the spirit. Without a doubt, united we stand, but only when all who are united in principle unite together in solidarity. The future does not lie in our hands, and therefore I make no promises to you. What I can be for you must become manifest to you not in words but in my ministry. In this manner, then, I accept that ministry, and in this manner I conclude this ceremony with my petition to the Holy One of Israel: that he not turn back my hand wherever it seeks to build up Jerusalem's walls. Amen.

---

2   Rev. C. S. Adama van Scheltema had published an *Open Letter to Dr. Kuyper*, in which he deplored Kuyper's conduct in Utrecht because it showed that "this talented man, this noble spirit," was in danger of becoming "an ecclesiastical Bismarck."

ABOUT ABRAHAM KUYPER

(1837–1920)

Abraham Kuyper's life began in the small Dutch village of Maassluis on October 29, 1837. During his first pastorate, he developed a deep devotion to Jesus Christ, spurring him to a deep commitment to Reformed theology, which profoundly influenced his later careers. He labored tirelessly, publishing two newspapers, leading a reform movement out of the state church, founding the Free University of Amsterdam, and serving as Prime Minister of the Netherlands. He died on November 8, 1920, after relentlessly endeavoring to integrate his faith and life; truly, his emphasis on worldview formation has had a transforming influence upon evangelicalism, through the diaspora of the Dutch Reformed churches and those they have inspired.

In the mid-nineteenth-century Dutch political arena, the increasing sympathy for the "No God, no master!" dictum of the French Revolution greatly concerned Kuyper. To desire freedom from an oppressive government or a heretical religion was one thing, but to eradicate religion from politics as spheres of mutual influence was, for Kuyper, unthinkable. Because man is sinful, he reasoned, a state that derives its power from men cannot avoid the vices of fallen human impulses. True limited government flourishes best when people recognize their sinful condition and acknowledge God's divine authority. In Kuyper's words, "The sovereignty of the state as the power that protects the individual and that defines the mutual relationships among the visible spheres, rises high above them by its right to command and compel. But within these spheres . . . another authority rules, an authority that descends directly from God apart from the state. This authority the state does not confer but acknowledges."

ABOUT THE CONTRIBUTORS

Nelson D. Kloosterman serves as Ethics Consultant for Worldview Resources International (St. John, Indiana, USA), a Christian service organization that provides resources for applying a Christian worldview to living in a global culture.

His earned degrees include a B.D. and a Th.D. For more than 25 years he taught, on the seminary level, courses in ethics, New Testament, and preaching. He has translated and published several books, including *The Ten Commandments: Manual for the Christian Life* and *Responsible Conduct: Principles of Christian Ethics* by J. Douma; *Preaching and the History of Salvation* by C. Trimp; and *Saved By Grace: The Holy Spirit's Work in Calling and Regeneration* by Herman Bavinck. His current Dutch-English translation projects include a 23-volume commentary, *Opening the Scriptures*, and co-translating and editing *Common Grace* and *Pro Rege*, the latter two by Abraham Kuyper.

Areas of interest include Christian medical ethics (beginning of life and end of life decisions), Christian business ethics, and the relationship between Christianity and culture in general. Personal hobbies include geocaching, chess, and motorcycling.

Harry Van Dyke (1940), who was taken from Holland to Canada at the age of 12, earned a B.A. at Calvin College and a D.Litt. at the VU Amsterdam. He has published a score of articles, numerous translations, and one book, *Groen van Prinsterer's Lectures* *on Unbelief and Revolution* (1989), besides editing anthologies of the writings of S. U. Zuidema and M. C. Smit.

For 12 years he served as research fellow and instructor in theory and philosophy of history at the VU Amsterdam, and then taught history in Redeemer University College for 23 years. Since his retirement he has given direction to the Dooyeweerd Centre for Christian Philosophy and has been involved in several translation projects. He and his wife have two adult daughters and two grandchildren, and they reside in Hamilton, Ontario, where they are members of one of five local Christian Reformed churches.

John Halsey Wood Jr. earned his Ph.D. in the history of Christian thought from Saint Louis University. He was also a Fulbright Scholar at the VU Amsterdam, Netherlands. He has written an award winning book titled *Going Dutch in the Modern Age: Abraham Kuyper's Struggle for a Free Church in the Nineteenth Century Netherlands* (New York: Oxford UP, 2013). He has also published a number of articles and book chapters on Abraham Kuyper's ecclesiology. He is serving as the general editor of the forthcoming *Abraham Kuyper Church Anthology.*

ABOUT THE KUYPER TRANSLATION SOCIETY

In 2011 a group of Abraham Kuyper scholars and experts met to form an association that has come to be known as the Abraham Kuyper Translation Society. Kuyper College and Acton Institute, along with other Abraham Kuyper scholars, have an interest in facilitating the translation of Abraham Kuyper's writings into English. Currently the society is involved in translating Kuyper's seminal three-volume work on common grace (*De gemeene gratie*), his three-volume work on the lordship of Christ (*Pro rege*), and key Kuyper texts on the church. The translated texts on the church will be published by Christian's Library Press in 2014 as an anthology.

The society recognizes that translations are not ends in themselves. Hence, plans are underway to produce an Abraham Kuyper Islam anthology that will focus on how deeply Kuyper's encounter with Islam toward the end of his life affected him and galvanized *Pro rege*, the last major work Kuyper completed in religion and theology. One anticipated result of translating Kuyper's writings on Islam is to reveal to twenty-first century Christians, particularly Christian students, how Kuyper successfully "engaged" another world religion and another culture. It is also hoped that this anthology, along with the translation of Kuyper's other writings, will enable Christians to draw on their Reformation heritage and develop a sense of vocation as wide as creation itself.

The society also exists to further additional Kuyper scholarly projects that will help promote a holistic vision of God's renewal encompassing all things.

Made in the USA
Middletown, DE
29 July 2019